Presented
to

AIMEE CRADDOCK

From

NAN

date 202

The Gift of
CHRISTMAS

Rev. JUDE WINKLER, OFM Conv.

Imprimi Potest: Mark Curesky, OFM Conv., Minister Provincial of St. Anthony of Padua Province (USA)
Nihil Obstat: James T. O'Connor, S.T.D., Censor Librorum
Imprimatur: ✠ **Patrick J. Sheridan, D.D.,** Vicar General, Archdiocese of New York

The Nihil Obstat and Imprimatur are official declarations that a book or pamphlet is free of doctrinal or moral error. No implication is contained therein that those who have granted the Nihil Obstat and Imprimatur agree with the contents, opinions or statements expressed.

CONTENTS

FOREWORD

CHRISTMAS is one of the greatest Christian feasts. It is also a most happy time. It is the day when we celebrate God's great love for us. We rejoice because God sent His only Son into our world to be born as a baby in Bethlehem.

Christmas takes its name from the expression "Christ's Mass." It recalls the Mass that the community offers to celebrate the birth of Jesus. The English language is unlike most of the other European languages in this. They give a name to this day that is based upon the words "to be born." Thus, in Latin we have *Dies Natalis;* in Italian, *Natale;* in Spanish *Navidad;* in French, the Latin form is softened into *Noel.*

This book is intended to help you celebrate Christmas with greater understanding, devotion, and joy. It is divided into three parts. (1) *Preparing for Christmas* shows how Jesus fulfilled the promises God made to the Chosen People. (2) *The Christmas Story* tells the story of the events that surrounded the birth of Jesus. (3) *Celebrating Christmas* shows the various customs with which Christmas is celebrated around the world.

May this book help all who use it to celebrate each Christmas more devoutly and more joyously with every passing year.

Part I: **PREPARING FOR CHRISTMAS**

THE SEASON OF ADVENT

S INCE Christmas is such an important day in our lives, there are many things we have to do to prepare for it.

Months before Christmas arrives we begin to think about the presents that we will receive from our parents. We must ask to go to the toy store or talk to our friends to decide what we should ask them to buy for us.

As the day approaches, there are all kinds of preparations to do at home. We help Dad and Mom get ready for our celebration.

We help them clean the house, bake cookies, decorate the Christmas tree, and all the other things that have to be done. There is really a lot to do to get ready for Christmas.

Yet, we have to be careful that we do not spend all our time preparing our homes and then forget to prepare our hearts. That is why we have a special time of the year called Advent.

The Season of Advent is when we look at our hearts to make sure that we are ready to welcome the baby Jesus into our lives and our love.

THE JESSE TREE

A DVENT is a good time to think back on how God prepared the hearts of His people for the birth of His only Son. That way, when we have heard how they grew closer to God all throughout their history, we might be encouraged to draw close to God ourselves.

It would be impossible to look at every single thing that God did for His people before Jesus was born, but maybe we can look at a few of those things.

We will be looking at the Jesse tree. This is the name given to the promises that God made throughout the Old Testament concerning the birth of His only Son.

Just like our Christmas tree, the Jesse tree has beautiful decorations. But instead of having stars and lights on it, it has the promises that God made to us and to His people, promises made out of love.

The tree is named after Jesse, the father of David, the great king of Israel. The reason for this is that some of the most important promises of all were made to Jesse and to his son David.

Among other things, they were promised that God's only Son would be born in their family.

DURING the Season of Advent we can think of the people and events of the Jesse Tree.

First Week — Numbers 1, 2, and 3
Second Week — Numbers 4, 5, and 6
Third Week — Numbers 7, 8, and 9
Fourth Week — Numbers 10 and 11

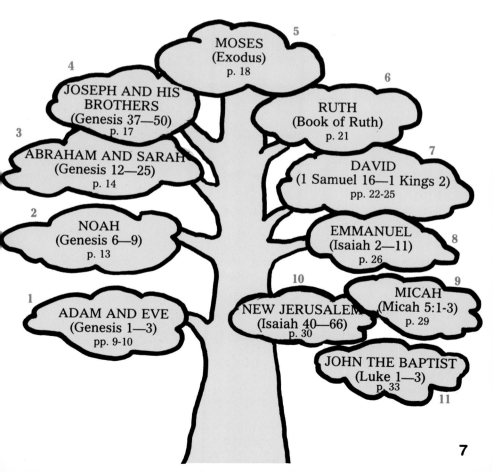

5
MOSES
(Exodus)
p. 18

4
JOSEPH AND HIS BROTHERS
(Genesis 37—50)
p. 17

6
RUTH
(Book of Ruth)
p. 21

3
ABRAHAM AND SARAH
(Genesis 12—25)
p. 14

7
DAVID
(1 Samuel 16—1 Kings 2)
pp. 22-25

2
NOAH
(Genesis 6—9)
p. 13

EMMANUEL
(Isaiah 2—11)
p. 26
8

10
NEW JERUSALEM
(Isaiah 40—66)
p. 30

MICAH
(Micah 5:1-3)
p. 29
9

1
ADAM AND EVE
(Genesis 1—3)
pp. 9-10

JOHN THE BAPTIST
(Luke 1—3)
p. 33
11

GOD CREATES ADAM AND EVE

THE first branch of this tree is very old, for it dates back all the way to the first days of the world.

In the beginning God created the heavens and the earth and all the things that are in them. The greatest of all the things that He created were the first man and woman. God loved Adam and Eve and He put them in charge of all His creation.

God placed Adam and Eve in the Garden of Eden. He told them that they could eat the fruit of any tree in the garden except the tree of the knowledge of good and evil. They were not to eat the fruit of that tree.

One day, while Eve was walking in the garden, a serpent spoke to her and convinced her to eat some of the fruit that she was not supposed to eat. When she had tasted the fruit, she gave some to Adam, her husband.

As soon as Adam and Eve had finished eating, they realized that they had sinned against God.

When God came to walk in the garden that evening, they hid from Him, for they knew that they had done something very bad. He called them out from hiding and spoke to them.

THE PROMISE OF A SAVIOR

WHEN they finally came out, God told the man, the woman, and the serpent that they would be punished for the bad thing they had done. He told the man that from then on he would have to work very hard to earn a living for his family. He told the woman that she would be punished by having much pain when she was giving birth to her children.

God gave the most serious punishment to the serpent for it had tempted the woman to turn against the Lord. He told it that it would no longer have any legs but would have to crawl on its belly for the rest of its life.

One part of the punishment is actually a promise to us. God told the serpent that the child of the woman would step on the head of the serpent. This was a promise that the devil would not be powerful forever. God was promising to send a Holy One who would crush the power of the evil one and free us from sin.

Then, to show us that He still loved Adam and Eve and all of us in spite of our sins, He made some clothes for Adam and Eve to protect them from the cold.

This is the story of God's first promise to send Jesus into the world.

NOAH AND THE FLOOD

IN spite of the love that God had shown Adam and Eve, men and women continued to turn against the Lord. They sinned more and more until God finally decided that He would have to punish the whole world.

God decided that He would send a great flood to destroy all life upon the earth. He would only save one very good family from the flood, Noah and his family.

One day God called to Noah and told him to build a large boat, an ark. When he was finished, he was to collect all kinds of animals and to put them on board the ark. Noah did just as the Lord commanded him.

When Noah was finished and had all the animals on board the ark, God sent a great flood that destroyed all people and animals upon the earth. The flood lasted a long time, but all throughout it God kept Noah and his family safe.

Then, when the flood was over, God promised Noah that He would never again flood the whole earth. He gave us the rainbow as a sign of His promise.

Once again, in spite of the fact that we had sinned, God gave us a sign of His mercy and His love.

ABRAHAM AND SARAH

THE next branch on our Jesse tree is the promise that God made to Abraham and Sarah. God promised that, even though they were very old, they would still have a son. Their children and grand-children and other descendants would be as many as the stars in the sky. He also promised them a fertile land in which they could dwell.

Abraham and Sarah waited for a long time, but still they had no children. Then, one day, God visited them along with two angels in the form of three desert travelers.

Abraham and Sarah were so kind and generous to them that God repeated His promise and then added that He would fulfill it within one year. Sarah soon became pregnant and gave birth to a son, Isaac.

Some time later, God asked Abraham to give Isaac back to Him in sacrifice. Although Abraham could have wondered whether God was taking back His promise, he trusted God.

When God saw Abraham's great faith, He stopped him from sacrificing his son and greatly re-warded Abraham and Sarah. They were to become the father and the mother of God's holy people, Israel. It would be to this people that God would send His only Son, Jesus.

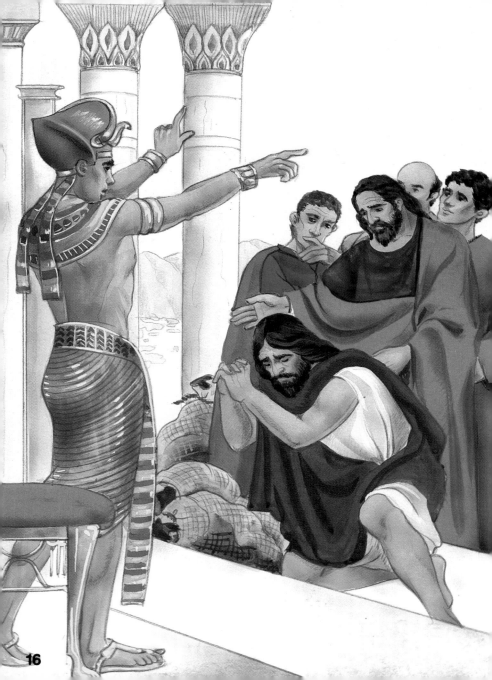

THE SONS OF JACOB

G OD continued to fulfill His promise to Abraham and Sarah. Isaac, their son, married Rebekah and they had two sons, Esau and Jacob. God chose Jacob as the son of His promise. Jacob and his wives, Leah and Rachel, had twelve sons and one daughter.

These twelve sons were to become the founders of the twelve tribes of Israel. Two of the most famous sons were Joseph and Judah.

Joseph was one of the youngest sons and he was a favorite of his father. His brothers hated him for that and sold him into slavery in Egypt. God cared for him there and made him an important official in the court of Pharaoh, the king of Egypt.

When a great famine broke out over all the earth, Joseph was able to give grain to his family and to save them from death. He forgave his brothers and brought them and their father Jacob to Egypt where they could live in safety.

Judah, the second oldest son, was to become famous because of a promise that Jacob made to his son before he died. He told Judah that he would be as strong as a lion and would be the father of great kings.

One day, the King of kings, Jesus, would be born from his tribe.

MOSES THE LIBERATOR

THE people of Israel grew very strong in Egypt, so strong that the Egyptians became frightened of them. They made them into slaves and treated them very badly.

God heard the cries of His people and He sent them a prophet, Moses, to lead them to freedom. Moses told Pharaoh to let his people go, and when Pharaoh refused, God sent a series of plagues against Egypt. Finally, God sent a terrible plague in which all the first sons of Egypt died, and Pharaoh let the people of Israel go.

When the army of Pharaoh chased after the people of Israel, God had Moses part the Red Sea and lead the people across. He drowned Pharaoh and his army in the Red Sea.

Israel dwelt in the desert for forty years. God cared for them there, giving them bread from heaven, which is called manna, and water from a rock. He also gave them a gift through Moses, the Ten Commandments, so that they would know how to serve God and to love each other.

Before he died, Moses promised that God would send another prophet greater than he ever was. That prophet was Jesus, God's only Son.

YOUR GOD WILL BE MY GOD

ONE of those who was part of God's promise was Ruth, a woman from a foreign land.

There was a good woman from Israel named Naomi who moved from her home in Bethlehem to Moab, a pagan land, with all of her family. While she was there, her two sons married women from Moab. Eventually her husband died as well as her two sons. She told her two daughters-in-law that they should return to their families and she would return to Jerusalem.

One of the daughters-in-law returned to her family, but Ruth, the other one, refused to do this. She told Naomi that she would go with her wherever she went. Naomi's people would be her people and Naomi's God would be her God.

Naomi and Ruth traveled to Bethlehem. When they arrived there, Ruth cared for Naomi by picking up the loose grain in the fields that had been harvested. God rewarded Ruth for her goodness to Naomi. He sent a good man of Israel, Boaz, into her life. They married and had a son named Obed, who was to be the grandfather of David, the great king of Israel.

Thus, Ruth was also one of the ancestors of Jesus, our Lord.

DAVID, THE SON OF JESSE

GOD does not always make the same choices that we would probably make, and this is seen most clearly in the story of David.

The people of Israel had asked God and the prophet Samuel for a king, and God had given them Saul. But Saul did things that were evil in the sight of God, so God told the prophet Samuel that he should go out and anoint a new king.

Samuel traveled to Bethlehem, to the house of Jesse, as God had ordered. He told Jesse to bring all his sons before him. But as each son passed in front of him, Samuel knew that the Lord was not choosing that man to be the future king of Israel.

When all Jesse's sons had passed in front of the prophet, Samuel asked Jesse if there were any others. Jesse said that the youngest son, David, was out tending sheep. Samuel had him called, and the minute he saw David he knew that God had chosen him.

God chose David not because he was the oldest or the tallest or the most handsome. He chose him because he was pure of heart, for God judges us according to our hearts. So Samuel took out his oil and anointed David the king of Israel.

A HOUSE FOR DAVID

DAVID became a great hero in Israel. He defeated the giant Goliath and many of the other enemies who were attacking his people. Then, when king Saul was killed in battle, David became the king of all of Israel.

One of the first things that David did as king was to capture the city of Jerusalem and to make it his capital. He built a great palace for himself. He also brought the Ark of the Covenant, the holiest of all the things that God had given to His people, into Jerusalem.

One day David called Nathan the prophet to his palace. David told Nathan that he felt guilty, for here he was living in a great palace while the Ark of the Covenant was still in a tent. He wanted to build a great temple to house the Ark.

God spoke to Nathan, sending him to speak to David. Nathan told David that God did not want him to build Him a house. Rather, God was going to give David a house that would never end.

This was a promise that David's descendants would rule over Israel for all time. It would be fulfilled when Jesus, the son of David, would become the King of Israel and the King of all kings.

EMMANUEL

THE descendants of David, however, did not follow the Lord with all their hearts. So God sent them prophets to call them back to His ways.

One of the prophets whom God sent was Isaiah. The people of Israel had sinned against the Lord and God had allowed their enemies to attack them. God then sent Isaiah to the king and told him to trust in the Lord, for God would defeat all of Israel's enemies.

Isaiah told the king to ask for a sign from the Lord as an assurance that they would be delivered, but the king refused to ask for a sign. The prophet told the king that God would give a sign anyway, for a maiden would bear a child who would be named Emmanuel, a name that means "God is with us."

The prophet also promised that when this child would reign, there would be a time a peace in Israel and over the whole world. The peace would be so great that even the wolf would lie down with the lamb and the lion with the calf. There would be a great peace on God's holy mountain.

Jesus, the Son of God, is the fulfillment of this promise, for He truly is "God with us"; He truly is the Prince of Peace.

LITTLE TOWN OF BETHLEHEM

S TILL the kings who lived in Jerusalem continued to sin against the Lord. And so God sent another prophet, Micah, who would make still another promise to the people of Israel.

Micah realized that the people of Jerusalem had forgotten the Lord. They were too rich and too important, so they did not have time to pray or to turn to the Lord. They were not humble enough to admit that they needed God's help.

But people of the small towns were always turning to God. Micah saw this and realized that the poor people and the unimportant are really the chosen ones of God. He remembered how God had chosen David, a rather small and unimportant child from Bethlehem, to be His great king.

So Micah spoke to Bethlehem and promised that another King would arise out of it. This King would reign over Israel just as David had done. He would be pleasing to God and turn all the people back to justice. He would rule forever.

When the Magi came to Herod to ask where the new King of Israel was born, the wise men of Israel turned to this promise to tell Herod that the Messiah was to be born in Bethlehem.

A NEW JERUSALEM

EVEN though God had sent many Prophets to Israel to turn His people away from their sins, they refused to listen to them. Finally, God sent a terrible punishment upon His people. He allowed the enemies of Israel to conquer the land and to take them off into exile.

The people of Israel were now living in a foreign land, and they began to wonder whether God had forgotten them or whether He was taking back His promises to them. God sent them a number of Prophets to reassure them that this was not the case.

These Prophets spoke of how God would restore His beloved land. He would build a new Jerusalem that would be much better than the one that had been destroyed. He would give His people a time of peace and prosperity.

God also promised that He would send one of His servants to His people. This Servant would preach the Word of God to all the nations and turn their hearts to the Lord. He would suffer for the sake of the people and take their sins upon Himself. He would die for His people, and then the Lord would raise Him from the dead.

That Servant of the Lord was Jesus Himself.

JOHN THE BAPTIST

THE people of Israel tried to believe in the promises that God had made, but they waited for a long time and suffered a great deal.

Then, one day, a priest named Zechariah was in the Temple burning incense before the altar of God. An angel appeared to him and told him that he and his wife, Elizabeth, would soon have a son.

They were to name their son John and he would be a powerful messenger of the Lord. He would turn the people back to the Lord and prepare them for the coming of the Messiah.

Zechariah and Elizabeth were both very old, and Zechariah wondered how this could happen. The angel Gabriel replied that he had been sent from God Himself. Because Zechariah had doubted the promise of the Lord, he would be unable to speak until the child was born.

Zechariah returned to his home and soon afterward Elizabeth became pregnant. The son whom Elizabeth was carrying was John the Baptist who would go out into the desert and baptize the people so that they might be ready to greet the Messiah with their whole hearts.

Part 2: THE CHRISTMAS STORY

THE EVENTS SURROUNDING
CHRIST'S BIRTH

DURING the Christmas Season, the Church celebrates the Birth of Jesus. Through the celebration of Mass, she brings before us all the events surrounding the coming of God's Son into the world.

These events begin with the announcement of Christ's birth by the angel to Mary and end with the finding of Jesus in the Temple. They are events that manifest God's marvelous power and His wonderful works as well as His great love for us.

It is good for us to think about these events, especially during this holy season. We can do so by reading the stories found in the following pages. They will help us know, love, and follow Jesus, our Lord, who came to bring God's grace to the world.

These events are also mysteries of our Faith. They enable us to grasp the main teaching that the Church stresses at the Christmas Season. Christ is the "Sun of Justice," who came to bring light, life, and joy to the human race, which was lost in darkness and sin.

By thinking of the events surrounding Christ's birth, we become filled with the true meaning of Christmas. Jesus is truly born in our hearts and in our love.

GOD SENDS HIS MESSENGER TO MARY

G OD loves the people of Israel in a very special
way. He promised that He would always be with
them to deliver them from the hands of their
enemies. He also promised to send them one who
would rule over them in His name.

The people eagerly awaited the birth of this
promised one. They called Him the Messiah, and
they expected Him to be a great King and a powerful
warrior. God, though, had a different plan.

His Messiah would be born as a poor and simple
one—for this Messiah would conquer evil not with
great armies but with the greatness of His love.

And so it was that God sent the angel Gabriel,
His messenger, to a young woman named Mary.
Mary was engaged to a man named Joseph, but they
had not yet begun to live together. Thus, she was still
a virgin.

The angel greeted Mary saying, "Hail Mary, full
of grace! The Lord is with you." Mary was confused
as to what this greeting meant, but Gabriel reassured
her that she had found favor with God. He told her,
"You will conceive and bear a son, and you shall
name Him Jesus." He then told her how great that
son would be.

Mary did not understand how she could have this child for she was still a virgin. But the angel said, "The Holy Spirit will come upon you and the power of the Most High will overshadow you. Therefore the child to be born will be called holy, the Son of God." The angel also said that Elizabeth, her cousin, was pregnant even though she was very old, for nothing was impossible for God.

Mary then answered, "Behold, I am the handmaid of the Lord. May it be done to me according to your word."

MARY VISITS ELIZABETH

B Y saying yes to the Lord's call, Mary was placing herself in great danger. She was engaged to Joseph, and he could have accused her of being unfaithful. He could have even had her put to death. But Mary trusted in the Lord.

Joseph, being a good man, decided that he would not have Mary punished in public. Instead, he would send her away quietly. But an angel visited him in a dream that night and explained to him that Mary had not been unfaithful. She was pregnant by the Holy Spirit. Joseph cared for Mary and took her to his home.

Mary was not worried about her own problems. She realized that her cousin, Elizabeth, was very old and that she would need her help. So Mary traveled in haste to the hill country of Judea to be with Elizabeth.

As soon as Elizabeth heard Mary's voice, she knew something very special had happened. The baby in her womb jumped for joy, and Elizabeth was filled with the Holy Spirit.

Elizabeth greeted Mary saying, "Most blessed are you among women, and blessed is the fruit of your womb." She asked how the mother of her Lord would come to visit her for she felt unworthy of so great an honor.

THE BIRTH OF JOHN THE BAPTIST

ELIZABETH also told Mary that she was sure Mary was blessed because she had trusted in what God had said to her through the angel.

Mary was filled with joy over all that had happened to her, and she answered Elizabeth by singing a song of praise to the Lord. She still found it difficult to believe that the Lord had chosen her, a weak and humble person, and had not chosen someone who was rich and powerful.

Mary stayed with her cousin Elizabeth for three months. At the end of that time, Elizabeth gave birth to a fine baby. On the eighth day after the baby was born, Elizabeth and Zechariah took him to be circumcised. When the elders asked her what name he was to be given, she said "John." The elders were confused for usually the child would be named after the father or grandfather. There was no one in their family named John.

They asked Zechariah what name the boy should be given. Now Zechariah had not been able to speak since the angel had spoken to him in the Temple to tell him about the future birth of his son. So Zechariah took a tablet and wrote the name John. At that very moment, he was healed and could once again speak. He praised the Lord for all the wonders He had worked.

JOSEPH AND MARY TRAVEL
TO BETHLEHEM

ABOUT this time, the Roman emperor called for a census. He wanted to find out how many people there were in his empire so that he could know how much they should pay him in taxes. Each man was to go back to the city of his birth with his whole family and register there.

So Joseph took Mary and they traveled from Nazareth where they were living to Bethlehem, the city of David. Joseph was a descendant of the great king David. Mary was in her ninth month, and it was a very difficult trip for her.

NO ROOM IN THE INN

THERE were so many people traveling that when Joseph and Mary looked for a place to spend the night, there was no room for them in the inn. They went from house to house, but no one had a place for them to stay.

Finally, one family took pity on them. There was no room for Joseph and Mary in their house, but they told them that they could stay in their stable. This stable was a cave where their animals would stay when the weather was cold, and Joseph and Mary would at least be warm there.

MARY GIVES BIRTH TO JESUS

JOSEPH took Mary to that cave outside of Bethlehem. They took some clean straw and made a bed. They made themselves as comfortable as possible.

It was not their home, but the great love and goodness that Joseph and Mary had was enough for them.

Mary's time came, and she gave birth to a son whom they would name Jesus, a name which means that Yahweh saves. This fulfilled all that the angel Gabriel had told Mary.

Mary took her baby son and wrapped Him in swaddling clothes, a kind of blanket. She and Joseph cleaned out one of the mangers, the place where the farmers would put hay for the animals. They put fresh straw in the manger and used it as a crib for their baby.

This was not the way the people believed that the Messiah would be born. They expected their king to be born in a palace and not in a stable.

Joseph gathered the animals and brought them close around the mother and child so that they would provide some warmth during the night. It seemed as if the animals realized what was happening and were praising the Lord.

THE ANGELS APPEAR TO THE SHEPHERDS

NEARBY there were some shepherds watching over their flocks. Shepherds in those days were not very nice persons. People did not trust them because they were afraid that the shepherds would rob something. For that reason, shepherds usually lived outside the cities, and people did not want to have them around.

Yet the very first people to whom the news of Jesus' birth was announced were these shepherds. An angel appeared to them, and all of a sudden they were surrounded by great lights. They were very frightened.

The angel reassured them and told them, "Do not be afraid; for behold, I proclaim to you good news of great joy that will be for all the people. For today in the city of David a savior has been born for you who is Messiah and Lord."

The angel then told the shepherds what they would see. He said that the child would be wrapped in swaddling clothes and lying in a manger. Suddenly there was a large number of angels singing and praising the Lord. The angels sang out,

"Glory to God in the highest
and on earth peace to people of good will."

47

THE SHEPHERDS GO TO WORSHIP
THE BABY

SUDDENLY, the angels vanished. The shepherds said, "Let us go to Bethlehem to see this thing which the Lord has made known to us."

They traveled in haste to Bethlehem to see the things that the angel had spoken of. When they arrived, they found everything just as the angel had promised. There before them was the baby wrapped in swaddling clothes and lying in a manger. They told Mary and Joseph everything that had happened to them that night.

THE SHEPHERDS PRAISE THE LORD

ALL the people who heard about what had happened to the shepherds, of how the angels had appeared and announced this great news to them, were filled with wonder. Mary kept all these things in her heart. She often wondered what all this meant.

After the shepherds had seen the babe and had given their gifts to Him and His parents, they went on their way. They returned to the fields where they were tending their sheep.

All the way home they kept talking among themselves about the wonders that they had seen that night. They praised the Lord because of all that He had done and especially because He had revealed these great things to them.

JESUS IS TAKEN TO THE TEMPLE

ON the eighth day after Jesus was born, Joseph and Mary took their baby to be circumcised. They gave Him the name Jesus, the name that the angel Gabriel had spoken to Mary.

Then, when it was time for Mary to be purified, they went up to the Temple in Jerusalem. Mary and Joseph brought along two turtle doves as an offering to the Lord. This was the offering that was to be made by people who were too poor to make a larger offering. They also brought along their baby, Jesus, who was now a little more than a month old.

There was an old man named Simeon in the Temple. The Holy Spirit had promised Simeon that he would not die until he saw the promised one of the Lord. As soon as he saw Jesus, Simeon knew that this baby was the Messiah.

Simeon thanked the Lord because He had kept His promise. He also told Mary that Jesus would be a reason for joy for many in Israel but that others would reject Him.

There was also an elderly woman worshiping in the Temple that day. This woman, Anna, was 84 years old. She came forward at that very moment and gave thanks to God for the child. She told everyone in Jerusalem about Him.

THE MAGI TRAVEL TO JERUSALEM

IN those days, there were people who would study the stars in order to find out what was going to happen in the future. One of the names given to these people was Magi. Many of them lived in the countries to the east of Israel.

Three of these Magi were looking at the skies when suddenly they saw a new star. They studied the star and realized that it was a sign that a new King had been born to the Jews.

The Magi set out from their own country in the east in order to meet that new King. They traveled with their servants and camels and the gifts that they were bringing to the baby.

This was a very dangerous trip, but the Magi knew that it was important for them to take the risk. They knew that this star was the sign of a most important King.

When the Magi arrived in Jerusalem, they looked around for information about the baby. They went up to many people and said, "Where is the newborn King of the Jews? We saw His star at its rising and have come to do Him homage." They were sure that everyone would know about Him, but it just was not so. No one whom they asked had heard anything about a newborn King.

THE MAGI MEET KING HEROD

S OON a report about these three Magi reached
king Herod, the king of the Jews. He was a very
evil man and had killed many people because he had
thought that they wanted to be king. When he heard
that the Magi were speaking about a newborn King,
he became frightened.

King Herod called the chief priests and the
scribes together and asked them about the promised
Messiah. He wanted to know where this Messiah
would be born.

The priests and scribes studied the question and
then told the king that the prophets had spoken
about how the Messiah would be born in Bethlehem,
the city of David. Bethlehem was called the city of
David because the great king of Israel had been born
there.

King Herod then called the Magi in to talk with
them in secret. He asked them when they had first
seen the star and many other things. When they had
answered all of his questions, he sent them away. He
told them to go to Bethlehem so that they could find
the child. When they had found Him, they were to
send word to king Herod for he told them that he
wanted to go and pay his respects to the child. However, he really wanted to kill Him.

THE MAGI WORSHIP THE CHILD

A S soon as the Magi set out, they once again saw the star. It was only about five miles from Jerusalem to Bethlehem, so the Magi were able to travel there in a short time.

When they arrived in Bethlehem, they saw that the star had stopped over a cave just outside the city. They went there and found Joseph, Mary, and the baby Jesus.

The Magi immediately entered the stable and fell down on their knees. They honored the child and brought out the gifts that they had brought Him from their homeland. They brought Him gifts of gold, frankincense, and myrrh.

It is said that there was a special meaning to these gifts, a meaning that even the Magi may not have realized when they chose them.

Gold was a gift that someone would give to a king. It is a sign of the fact that Jesus is the King of the Jews and the King of all kings. Frankincense is a type of incense. One would normally burn it as an offering to God. It was a sign of the hidden fact that Jesus is the only Son of God. Finally, myrrh is an ointment that one would use when someone was being buried. It pointed to the way that Jesus would free us from our sins, through His death and resurrection.

THE FLIGHT INTO EGYPT

THE Magi were going to go back to Jerusalem to tell king Herod about the child, but an angel appeared to them in a dream and told them to go back a different way.

When they had left, this angel spoke to Joseph in a dream as well. He warned him that king Herod was seeking to harm the child. The angel told Joseph to take Jesus and His mother and to flee to Egypt.

Joseph woke up Mary and they gathered together everything that they had and set out for Egypt with the baby Jesus that very night. There the baby would be safe from the evil king Herod. What they did also fulfilled what one of the prophets had said long ago, "Out of Egypt I called my son."

King Herod waited for the Magi to return back to him and give him a report about the child, but it soon became clear that they were not going to come back. He sent out his soldiers with the order that they were to kill all the baby boys who lived anywhere around Bethlehem who were two years old or younger.

The soldiers went throughout the town and the surrounding countryside and killed every small baby boy they found. They showed no mercy in spite of the cries of the mothers.

THE RETURN TO NAZARETH

A short time later Joseph and Mary heard the report that the evil king Herod had died. They knew it would now be safe for them to leave their refuge in Egypt and take their baby back to their home.

When Joseph and Mary set out, they heard that Herod's son, Archelaus, was now ruling in Jerusalem. They also heard that he was even a worse man than his father.

Joseph and Mary knew that their baby would be in great danger if they went back to Bethlehem. Therefore they did not want to return there.

Joseph and Mary decided that they would travel back to Nazareth, the city where they had been living before the census. There they would certainly be safe from everything that might harm them.

And so Joseph and Mary took their child Jesus and made the long journey back to the village of Nazareth.

When they arrived there, Joseph set up a house for his family. He had always been a carpenter, and now he was able to have a small shop in which he could do his work and earn a living for his family.

JESUS GROWS IN GRACE AND WISDOM

JESUS grew up big and strong, but He also grew in grace and wisdom. In so many ways He was like all the other boys of the village. Yet there was something special about Him.

Mary sewed His clothes, prepared His food, and watched over Him. She saw how He helped her around the house and her husband in the carpenter shop. He looked so normal.

And yet she knew He was special for she had received the message from the angel. This must have been very confusing for Mary. But she kept praying, and she placed her trust in the Lord.

JESUS HELPS IN THE CARPENTER SHOP

L IKE the other children of His time, Jesus probably attended school at the synagogue. There He would learn a little about reading and writing, geography and history, all by reading the stories of the Bible.

Jesus would also have learned some important lessons at home. Joseph was a carpenter, and he probably taught Jesus all about the work that he did.

Jesus probably also learned much from Mary His mother. She showed Him how to trust in the Lord, for she had done this in her own life.

JESUS IS LOST IN THE TEMPLE

JOSEPH and Mary were very good Jews, and each year they would travel up to Jerusalem for the great feast of Passover. When Jesus was twelve years old, the age at which a Jewish boy became a man, they took Him up with them.

After the feast, Joseph and Mary set out to return to Nazareth. They looked around for Jesus, but they could not find Him. At first they thought He was in another part of the camp. But when they came to rest that evening and still did not find Him, they realized He was lost.

Joseph and Mary returned to Jerusalem and looked for Jesus for three days. They went up to the Temple and searched for Him there.

His parents were most surprised when they found Jesus sitting in the Temple and speaking with the elders. He was listening to their teaching and asking them questions.

Mary went up to Jesus and asked Him, "Son, why have You done this to us? Your father and I have been looking for You."

Jesus answered her, "Why were you looking for Me? Did you not know that I must be in My Father's house?" He then returned with Mary and Joseph and stayed in Nazareth until the day that He began His preaching.

Part 3: CELEBRATING CHRISTMAS

CHRISTMAS DAY

I N the early days of the Church, no one was sure of when Jesus was born. So Christians in Rome chose to celebrate His birth on December 25, because the pagans already had a feast on that day when they celebrated the birth of the sun. This way, they might convince some of the pagans to become Christians. So we too celebrate Christmas on December 25.

For many of us Christmas is the happiest day of the year. It is a wonderful day when we celebrate the birth of our Lord Jesus Christ. In the weeks before Christmas, we decorate our Christmas tree and bake cookies and prepare a list of those things for which we will ask and those things we would like to give to our parents and brothers and sisters. Then on Christmas Day we go to Mass to begin our Christmas Day with God. When we arrive home, we open our Christmas presents and eat our Christmas meal.

Most of all, Christmas is a day to remember God's great love for us. We join with people from all over the world to thank Him for sending His only Son to be born as a baby in Bethlehem. But why do we do certain things to celebrate Christmas? Why do we have Christmas trees and Christmas cards? Why do we prepare a manger set? And who is Santa Claus and how does he belong to our Christmas celebrations?

THE CHRISTMAS TREE

A NOTHER Christmas custom that Christians have borrowed from the pagans is the Christmas tree. This custom was first practiced in Germany in the eighth century after Christ.

St. Boniface, a priest from England, had traveled to Germany to try to convert the pagans there. He had met with some success, but he was having a problem because many of the German people still wanted to worship their pagan gods.

St. Boniface wondered how he could convince the German people that the sacred oak worshiped by them was not a god. He finally decided that he would go into the forest and cut the sacred oak down.

The pagans were very angry when they heard of what St. Boniface had done. Now St. Boniface had to worry about how he would be able to calm them down.

Finally, he decided to give them a young evergreen tree as a sign of what Jesus was offering them. Unlike the oak that lost its leaves every year, the evergreen did not lose its leaves at all. This would be a sign of the life that Jesus was offering, a life that would never end.

For the German people and for us, the Christmas tree is an important reminder of the gift God offers us in His Son: everlasting life.

HOLLY

IVY

MISTLETOE

CHRISTMAS PLANTS

THERE are also other plants associated with Christmas. Three of them come from England: holly, ivy, and mistletoe.

Holly has been used for hundreds of years to make wreaths that were hung on the doors of homes and in churches. Among some people, it was believed that holly had magical powers, for it was said to be able to keep witches away. But even more important is the fact that it was always seen as a reminder of the crown of thorns that Jesus wore when He was crucified. It is said that the red berries represent drops of blood that fell from Jesus' head.

Ivy has both a good and a bad meaning. For some, it was a sign of the pagan religions (for it is often made into crowns that were placed on the statues of pagan gods). The holly and the ivy were opposed (Christianity and paganism), and the holly won. Yet some speak of the white berries of the ivy as being a sign of purity and innocence.

The third plant, the *mistletoe,* had been used by the Celtic Druids (pagan priests) even before Christians arrived. They considered it to be sacred and used it in their ceremonies. So it was forbidden to use it in Christian churches. Yet it was often used in homes, for it was a charm to bring on marriage. To this day, there is a custom that one can kiss a person who is standing under a sprig of mistletoe.

THE YULE LOG

MANY other customs developed during the Middle Ages to celebrate this holy day. Some of them are still practiced, but others have slowly given way to newer ways of celebrating Christmas.

One of these customs is the Yule log. After the harvest, the workers on the great estates would go into the woods to find a great, thick tree trunk. They would cut it down and take home its widest part. When they arrived at the noble's house, they would soak the log in water to make it as wet as possible.

On Christmas Eve, the log would be taken into the noble's house and put in the fireplace. They would light a small fire under it, keeping the fire burning at all times. Because the log was huge and very wet, it would take a long time for the log to catch on fire and burn. As long as a part of that log had not yet burned, the workers did not have to go back to their work. It would take about a week for the whole log to burn.

Another medieval custom was to have a Christmas joust. All the Knights from a region would gather and practice their skills against one another as part of their Christmas festivities.

Finally, because Christmas was so holy, it was forbidden to do battle on Christmas and in the days surrounding it, for Christ is the prince of peace.

74

THE CHRISTMAS CRIB

ST. Francis of Assisi gave us one of the most beautiful Christmas customs. One December, St. Francis was staying in a cave on a hillside outside of a small town named Greccio. He always had a great love for Christmas and he wanted to help the townspeople celebrate it in a special way that year.

He asked permission of the Holy Father to put on a kind of Christmas play. St. Francis told the people of the town to bring their animals—their donkeys, sheep, and oxen—to the cave where he was staying. He also set up a crib as there had been in Bethlehem. Then the people celebrated their Midnight Mass to welcome in Christmas day.

During the Mass, St. Francis, who was a deacon, proclaimed the Gospel. He was so filled with love that the people who were there saw a vision in which St. Francis reached down and picked up the Baby Jesus, whom they saw as alive and real.

All of the people overflowed with joy and love at this great event, and it was said that they did not even need their torches to find their way home that night, for they were glowing with love.

The friars who followed St. Francis have spread the custom of setting up Christmas manger scenes all over the world.

CHRISTMAS CARDS

ANOTHER Christmas custom with which we are very familiar is the Christmas card. It is a great joy to send out these greetings and to hear from people whom we love but might not have seen for quite a while.

The earliest Christmas cards go all the way back to the fifteenth century. They were sheets of paper with the Christmas story printed on them, and they were not really the same things as the Christmas cards that we now send.

The first true Christmas card was printed in Britain in 1843 by Henry Cole. The center of the design is a Christmas feast with two scenes printed on either side of it that show Christians doing acts of charity. The card sent wishes for "A Merry Christmas and A Happy New Year to you." This first card was not very successful.

In the United States, one of the first Christmas cards was produced by Louis Prang in Boston in 1875. It was an immediate success.

Today, hundreds of millions of Christmas cards are sent each year. Some have pictures of the crib at Bethlehem or of Mary holding the Baby Jesus; others show a Christmas tree or a winter scene. But they all wish the people to whom we send them the joy of Christmas.

SILENT NIGHT

CHRISTMAS CAROLS

A LONG with Christmas cards, Christmas carols are one of the warmest memories that most of us have at Christmas time. In many cities, people still go from house to house, singing these simple songs that come from Europe and America. We hear their melodies in stores as we shop in the month of December. Every Christmas special on TV has our favorite singer or a chorus singing these wonderful songs. Then they are sung by the whole community as we gather for our Christmas Masses on Christmas Day and in the weeks after Christmas.

One of the most beautiful of these songs is "Silent Night, Holy Night." It was written almost by accident. Father Joseph Mohr, a priest from a small village in Austria, was getting his church ready for Christmas Midnight Mass in 1818. He discovered that the Church organ would not work. The mice had eaten out the cloth parts of the organ and it would not play.

Father Mohr was worried that there would be no music for Christmas. So he asked the schoolmaster, Franz Gruber, to set a Christmas poem he had written to music. Gruber worked on the song for the rest of the day, and then that night they sang their song, "Silent Night," to the music that he played on Father Mohr's new guitar. That night, Franz Gruber's wife turned to him and said, "I am proud of you! People will sing your carol long after we both are dead."

GOOD KING WENCESLAUS

A NOTHER beautiful carol that we sing at Christmas time has little to do with the Christmas story itself. The carol is "Good King Wenceslaus," and it speaks about a king who ruled long ago in Bohemia, which today is a part of Czechoslovakia.

Wenceslaus was born just about the time when the Catholic faith had arrived in Bohemia. His grandparents were both Catholic as was his father, but his mother, although she was baptized, really believed in the pagan ways. When his father, the king, died Wenceslaus was twelve years old—too young to be king. His grandmother cared for him for a while, but his mother had her put to death and tried to make him into a pagan. Yet the boy continued to read the Bible in secret and sneaked priests into the palace to teach him.

When he was eighteen Wenceslaus became king. He ruled in a wise and just manner. He was famous for treating the simple people with respect and helping them. Often, when someone owed so much money that he and his family were about to be sold as slaves, he would pay their debts himself.

After Wenceslaus had ruled for only two years, the pagan nobles and his own brother plotted against him and had him killed. Yet the people so loved their king that they never forgot him and to this day they sing of their beloved good king Wenceslaus.

ST. LUCY

A NOTHER Saint who is associated with Christmas is St. Lucy. Her memory is especially celebrated in Sweden where her feast day, December 13, is a special holiday.

St. Lucy lived in Sicily in southern Italy during the days of one of the last Roman emperors who persecuted Christians. She is said to have hidden her fellow Christians underground in the catacombs (the name of the tunnels where they would bury the dead).

Every night Lucy would climb down to bring them food. In order to be able to carry more food, she would carry her oil lamps on her head. Eventually, she was caught and put to death for being a Christian.

Her story was told in many countries, and in Sweden she became especially popular. They were very impressed with her service of others. The Swedes would speak of how her head was surrounded with a halo of light.

To celebrate her feast, a young daughter from each family gets up very early on December 13 and dresses up in a long white robe with a red sash around her waist. She puts on a crown of ivy that has seven candles in it. Then she wakes everybody up and serves them coffee and baked goods.

SANTA CLAUS

A ND what would Christmas be without Santa Claus. Originally, Santa Claus, like St. Wenceslaus and St. Lucy, was a saint. His name was St. Nicholas, and he was a bishop of a city named Myra in Turkey. He lived in the early part of the fourth century and died on December 6 or 7 in the middle of the fourth century.

The most famous story told about St. Nicholas has to do with three young sisters who were very poor. Their parents were so poor that they did not have enough money for the daughters to get married.

Nicholas heard about this and wanted to help them, but he did not want anyone to know that he was the one who was helping them.

Here the story is told in a few different ways. In one of the versions, he climbed up on their roof three nights in a row and threw gold coins down their chimney so that they would land in the girls' stockings, which had been hung by the fire to dry.

When the Dutch settlers came to the new world, they also brought their devotion to "Sinter Klaus" (St. Nicholas). In their legends, he was no longer pictured as being thin, but he began to look more and more like the Santa Claus that we know, with a jolly red face and a white beard.

THE "BEFANA"

C HRISTMAS customs are very different all over the world. While we speak of Santa Claus visiting our homes on Christmas Eve and dropping down our chimneys to leave us presents (as St. Nicholas did), other nations have different traditions about Christmas presents and who brings them.

In Italy, for example, Christmas is not even the day on which people receive presents. There, as in many other nations, presents are received on the feast of the Epiphany, January 6.

The Epiphany is the day when we celebrate the visit of the three Magi who came from the East to visit the Baby Jesus. They brought gifts of gold, frankincense, and myrrh with them to give honor to the newborn King of the Jews. Thus, it makes sense to give and receive gifts on that day to remember what the three Magi did.

In Italy, though, there is an interesting twist on the story. There, a good witch named the "Befana," visits everyone's home. Like Santa Claus, she knows who has been naughty and who has been nice. She brings gifts to all of the children who have been good throughout the year, but she leaves coal for those who have been bad. Her name, the "Befana," comes from the name of the feast on which she brings her gifts ("Epifania" in Italian).

THE "POSADAS"

IN Mexico, in the meantime, the nine days before Christmas Day are filled with Christmas celebrations. These days are called the "posadas," the Spanish word for lodgings or inns. Each of these meals stands for one of the inns in which Joseph and Mary stopped on their way to Bethlehem.

The evening begins as darkness falls. The children of the neighborhood carry three small statues: one of Mary on a donkey, one of Joseph, and one of an angel who is following them. The children all take a candle and sing hymns while they march in procession to the nearest house.

When they reach the house, they knock on the door and ask if Mary and Joseph can stay there for the night. If this is not the house for the "posada," they are told that everyone is asleep and they must go away. Finally, when they reach the chosen house, they are let in. They set up an altar decorated with their candles and flowers and they begin their nightly celebration.

There is food and music and dancing each of the nine nights of the "posadas." There is also a "pinata," a clay figure filled with candy and toys, which is broken open each night. A child is blindfolded and given a stick. The child tries to break the figure, and when it is broken, treats fall out and all the children rush to get their fill of the candy and other treats.

THE "OPLATEK"

WE have spoken of a number of Christmas customs, but there is one other thing that reminds us of Christmas: food. Christmas is a time when we come together as a family and share a large supper with many wonderful types of food.

Each nation has its own traditions that involve food. In England, for example, people eat goose and plum pudding. In Italy, there is a special coffee cake named the "Panettone" and a candy filled with nuts called "Torrone." In America, we have our Christmas cookies and fruitcake. Many families also have either ham or turkey for dinner on Christmas Day.

One beautiful custom involving food is found in Poland. There people bake pieces of bread that look almost like the hosts we use at Mass. They are called "oplatek," and each piece has a holy picture pressed upon its surface.

In the old days, people would carry their "oplatek" from house to house and wish their neighbors a Merry Christmas. Today, the bread is mostly shared with members of the family and immediate neighbors.

As each person shares the bread, he or she is asked to do two things: forgive any hurts that have occurred over the past year and wish the person all the possible happiness in the coming year.

CHRISTMAS IN THE ORIENT

IN many parts of the world, it is not easy to celebrate Christmas. In countries where the government is communist, it is often illegal to take off from work on December 25.

Then, in other countries, Christians are only a small minority. In Japan, there are only about one half a million Christians in a country of 170 million people. Thus, many people do not even understand the meaning of Christmas. Christians use the holy day to tell their friends the story of Jesus.

In India, likewise, there are few Christians in comparison to the population. Yet the Christians of India have an advantage, for the Hindus, the major religion of India, have a Festival of Light called "Diwali," and Christians can use this festival as an example of what Christmas is like. In fact, they use some of the customs of that feast and other customs from the West to celebrate their Christmas.

One of the aspects of their Christmas celebration is also their Christmas Day service. It is a long service, usually lasting from two to three hours. The churches are filled with candles and flowers and the bright colored clothes of all the people.

In some parts of India, too, people go from house to house singing Christmas carols all the night long.

THE TRUE MEANING OF CHRISTMAS

AS we read through these Christmas customs, we should be able to recognize some of the things that we do in our own country and some things that seem unusual to us. Because our ancestors have come from all over the world, we often have a mixture of customs that we follow — some from our own family and others from the families of friends.

One of the things that many people have complained about in recent years is that Christmas has become too commercial. People are worried about presents and cards and all the other preparations, but they forget the real meaning of Christmas. It is the birth of the Baby Jesus, God's message of love to each one of us.

Christmas should be spent in a way that reminds us of that message. We should tell the story of the birth of Jesus and sing about it in our carols. We should remember the true meaning of our Christmas tree and our manger sets. We should say a quick prayer every time we wish someone a Merry Christmas.

We should thank God for our families and remember that they are God's greatest gift to us. We should also remember those who are not as fortunate as we are because they are poor or homeless, and maybe we should think of sharing some of our gifts with them.

CHRISTMAS EVERY DAY

AFTER seeing all these customs from around the world, we can see there are many, many ways to celebrate Christmas. Whatever we do, it should help to remind us that Jesus cares so much for us that He was born in a manger out of love for us.

We, like St. Francis, should be so on fire with love for God that everyone can see that Jesus is real and alive in our hearts. We should make every day a little Christmas.

Other Great Books for Children

FIRST MASS BOOK—Ideal Children's Mass Book with all the official Mass prayers. Colored illustrations of the Mass and the Life of Christ. Confession and Communion Prayers.   Ask for No. 808

The STORY OF JESUS—By Father Lovasik, S.V.D. A large-format book with magnificent full colored pictures for young readers to enjoy and learn about the life of Jesus. Each story is told in simple and direct words.   Ask for No. 535

CATHOLIC PICTURE BIBLE—By Rev. L. Lovasik, S.V.D. Thrilling, inspiring and educational for all ages. Over 110 Bible stories retold in simple words, and illustrated in full color.   Ask for No. 435

LIVES OF THE SAINTS—New Revised Edition. Short life of a Saint and prayer for every day of the year. Over 50 illustrations. Ideal for daily meditation and private study.   Ask for No. 870

PICTURE BOOK OF SAINTS—By Rev. L. Lovasik, S.V.D. Illustrated lives of the Saints in full color. It clearly depicts the lives of over 100 popular Saints in word and picture.   Ask for No. 235

Saint Joseph CHILDREN'S MISSAL—This new beautiful Children's Missal, illustrated throughout in full color. Includes official Responses by the people. An ideal gift for First Holy Communion.
    Ask for No. 806

St. Joseph FIRST CHILDREN'S BIBLE—By Father Lovasik, S.V.D. Over 50 of the best-loved stories of the Bible retold for children. Each story is written in clear and simple language and illustrated by an attractive and superbly inspiring illustration. A perfect book for introducing very young children to the Bible.   Ask for No. 135

WHEREVER CATHOLIC BOOKS ARE SOLD